TO ELIZABETH, MIKE, STEVE, EDDY AND TERRY

FOR ALL THEIR HELP AND ENCOURAGEMENT

First published 1993 by Walker Books Ltd, 87 Vauxhall Walk, London SE11 5HJ

This Special New Edition published 1997

This edition produced 2000 for The Book People Ltd
Hall Wood Avenue, Haydock, St Helens WA11 9UL

2 4 6 8 10 9 7 5 3 1

© 1993, 1997 Martin Handford

Printed in Hong Kong

British Library Cataloguing in Publication Data
A catalogue record for this book is available from the British Library.

ISBN 0-7445-5539-6

WHERE'S WALLY? IN HOLLYWOOD

MARTIN HANDFORD

TED SMART

A DREAM COME TRUE

WOW, WALLY-WATCHERS, THIS IS FANTASTIC, I'M REALLY IN HOLLYWOOD! LOOK AT THE FILM PEOPLE EVERYWHERE – I WONDER WHAT MOVIES THEY'RE MAKING. THIS IS MY DREAM COME TRUE ... TO MEET THE DIRECTORS AND ACTORS, TO WALK THROUGH THE CROWDS OF EXTRAS, TO SEE BEHIND THE SCENES! PHEW, I WONDER IF I'LL APPEAR IN A MOVIE MYSELF!

★ ★ ★ WHAT TO LOOK FOR IN HOLLYWOOD! ★ ★ ★

WELCOME TO TINSELTOWN, WALLY-WATCHERS! THESE ARE THE PEOPLE AND THINGS TO LOOK FOR AS YOU WALK THROUGH THE FILM SETS WITH WALLY.

★ FIRST (OF COURSE!) WHERE'S WALLY?

★ NEXT FIND WALLY'S CANINE COMPANION, WOOF – REMEMBER, ALL YOU CAN SEE IS HIS TAIL!

★ THEN FIND WALLY'S FRIEND, WENDA!

★ ABRACADABRA! NOW FOCUS IN ON WIZARD WHITEBEARD!

★ BOO! HISS! HERE COMES THE BAD GUY, ODLAW!

★ NOW SPOT THESE 25 WALLY-WATCHERS, EACH OF WHOM APPEARS ONLY ONCE BEFORE THE FINAL FANTASTIC SCENE!

★ WOW! INCREDIBLE! SPOT ONE OTHER CHARACTER WHO APPEARS IN EVERY SCENE EXCEPT THE LAST!

★ ★ KEEP ON SEARCHING! THERE'S MORE TO FIND! ★ ★

ON EVERY SET FIND WALLY'S LOST KEY!

WOOF'S LOST BONE! ★ WENDA'S LOST CAMERA! ★ WIZARD WHITEBEARD'S SCROLL!

ODLAW'S LOST BINOCULARS! ★ AND A MISSING CAN OF FILM!

★ ★ ★ ★ ★ ★ ★ AND MORE AND MORE! ★ ★ ★ ★ ★ ★ ★

EACH OF THE FOUR POSTERS ON THE WALL OVER THERE IS PART OF ONE OF THE FILM SETS WALLY IS ABOUT TO VISIT. ★ FIND OUT WHERE THE POSTERS CAME FROM. ★ THEN SPOT ANY DIFFERENCES BETWEEN THE POSTERS AND THE SETS.

SHHH! THIS IS A SILENT MOVIE

SO THIS IS HOW THE HOLLYWOOD DREAM BEGAN – WITH SILENT MOVIES MADE IN BLACK AND WHITE. IT LOOKS CRAZY AND IT MAKES YOU LAUGH. ACTING IN SLAPSTICK COMEDIES MUST BE REALLY HARD – LOOK HOW MANY ACCIDENTS ARE HAPPENING. BUT THE GREAT THING IS THAT NONE OF THE ACTORS EVER GET HURT, HOWEVER OFTEN THEY FALL FLAT ON THEIR FACES!

$10,000

HORSEPLAY IN TROY

WHAT A SPECTACULAR SCENE THIS IS, WALLY-WATCHERS! AND WHAT AN EPIC COMMOTION PICTURE! I WONDER WHY THE TROJANS DIDN'T GUESS THE WOODEN HORSE WAS FULL OF GREEKS, AND HOW DID THEY GET IT THROUGH THE GATES OF TROY ANYWAY? I WOULDN'T LIKE TO BE IN THE TROJANS' SANDALS, IF THE COSTUME DEPARTMENT HAD GIVEN THEM ANY, THAT IS!

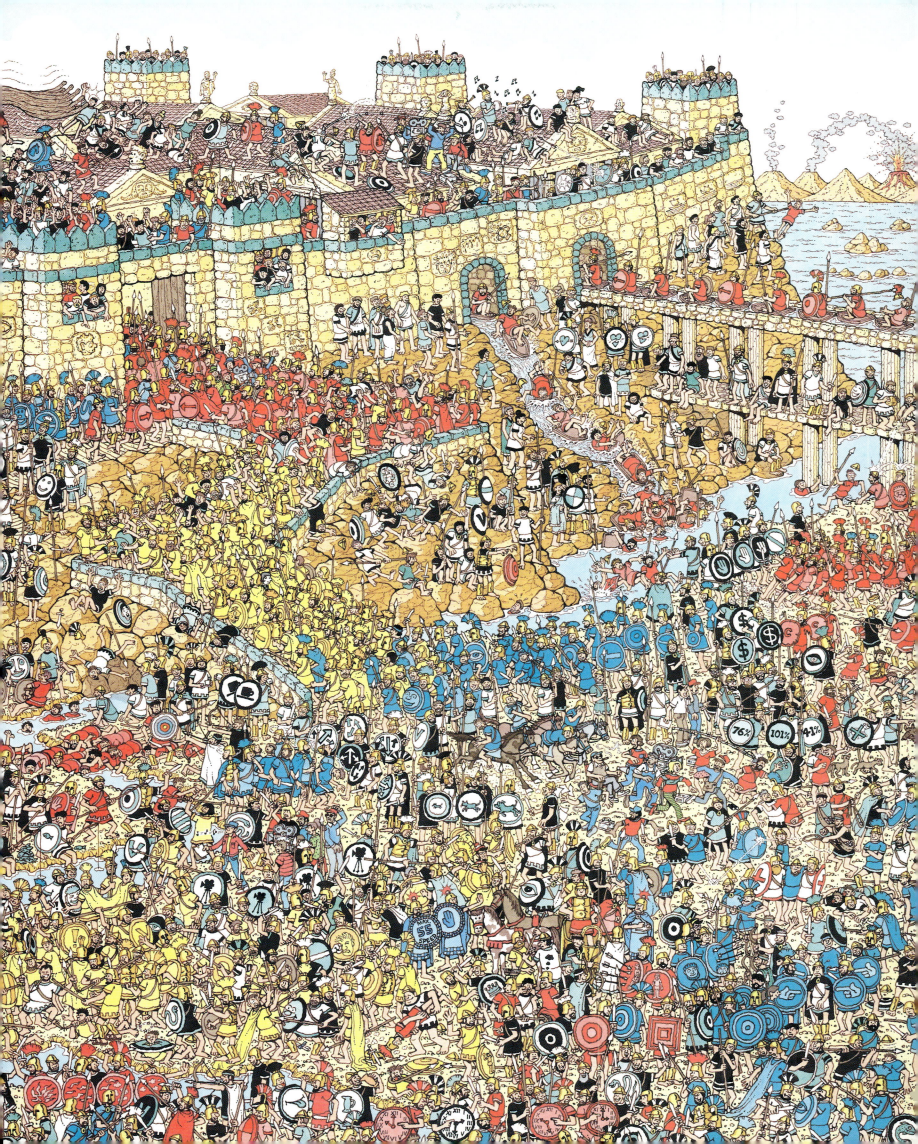

FUN IN THE FOREIGN LEGION

PHEW, FILM FANS, DON'T GET OVERHEATED, THIS IS THE MOST SIZZLING LOCATION SO FAR! EVERYONE'S SWELTERING, FROM STARS TO SAND-SHIFTERS. SOME OF THOSE EXTRAS LOOK LIKE THEY'RE LOSING THEIR COOL – HAVE THEY FORGOTTEN THIS IS ONLY A FILM? PERHAPS IT'S TIME A FEW MORE OF THEM DESERTED THE DESERT AND JOINED THE RUSH FOR ICE-CREAM!

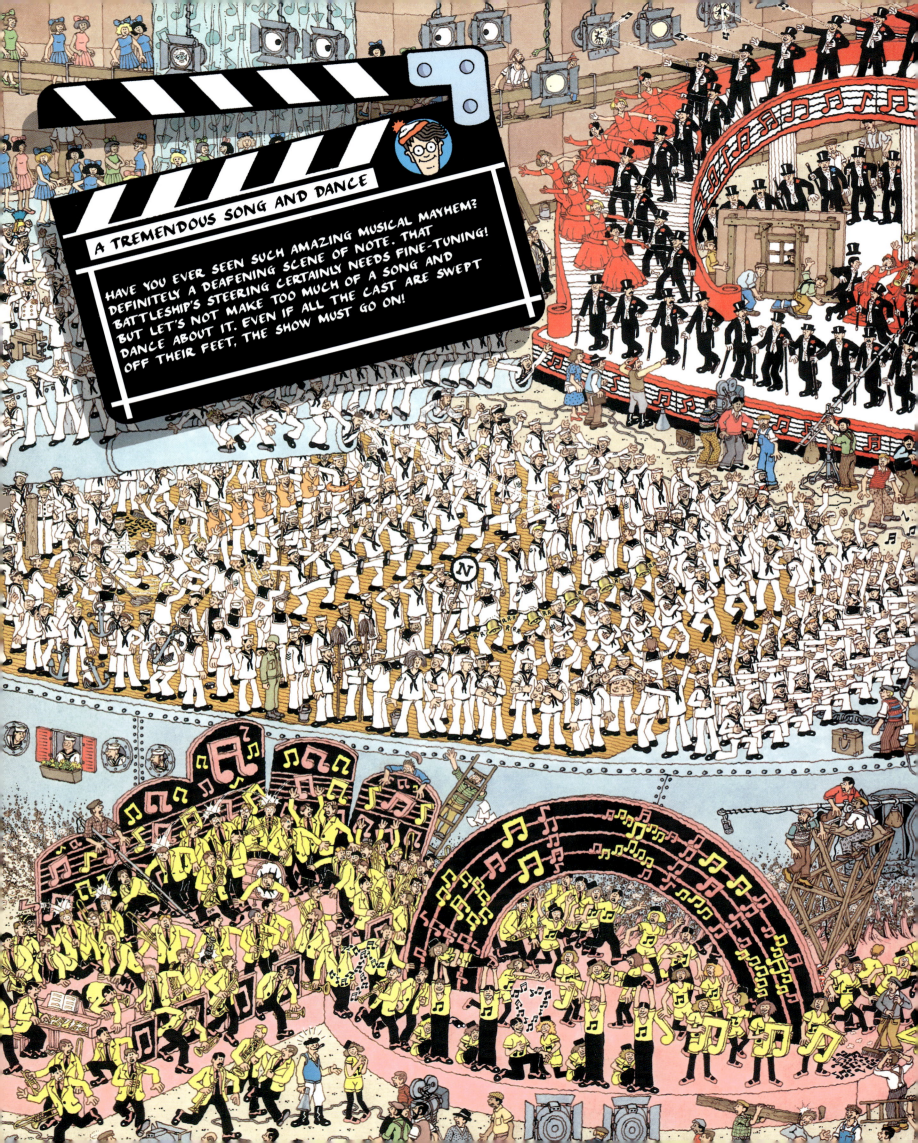

A TREMENDOUS SONG AND DANCE

HAVE YOU EVER SEEN SUCH AMAZING MUSICAL MAYHEM?
DEFINITELY A DEAFENING SCENE OF NOTE. THAT
BATTLESHIP'S STEERING CERTAINLY NEEDS FINE-TUNING!
BUT LET'S NOT MAKE TOO MUCH OF A SONG AND
DANCE ABOUT IT. EVEN IF ALL THE CAST ARE SWEPT
OFF THEIR FEET, THE SHOW MUST GO ON!

ALI BABA AND THE FORTY THIEVES

WHAT A CRUSH IN THE CAVE, WALLY-FOLLOWERS, BUT
PAN IN ON THOSE POTS OF TREASURE! HOW MANY
THIEVES WERE IN THE STORY? I BELIEVE THIS DIRECTOR
THINKS FORTY THOUSAND! HAVE YOU SPOTTED ALI BABA?
HE'S IN THE ALLEY, CUTTING HAIR — THE SCRIPTWRITER
THINKS HIS NAME'S ALLEY BARBER! JANGLING GENIES —
WHAT A FEARFULLY FUNNY FLICK THIS IS!

THE SWASHBUCKLING MUSKETEERS

ALL FOR ONE, ONE FOR ALL! – WASN'T THAT THE
MOTTO OF THE THREE MUSKETEERS? NOW LOOK
AT THIS FREE-FOR-ALL! CAN YOU SPOT OUR THREE
GALLANT HEROES BATTLING WITH THE RED-COATED
CARDINAL'S GUARDS? WITH ALL THIS SWASHBUCKLING
ACTION GOING ON, I WONDER HOW THE CAMERAMEN
CAN CAPTURE IT ALL ON FILM!

DINOSAURS, SPACEMEN AND GHOULS

PHEW, INCREDIBLE! TIME, SPACE AND HORROR ARE IN A MIGHTY MUDDLE HERE! WHAT COSMIC COSTUMES AND WHAT GREAT SPECIAL EFFECTS! ONE OF THOSE FLYING SAUCERS LOOKS LIKE IT'S REALLY FLYING! ARE THOSE REAL ALIENS INSIDE, NOT ACTORS AT ALL? SO WHAT'S REAL AND WHAT'S MADE UP IN FILMS LIKE THESE?

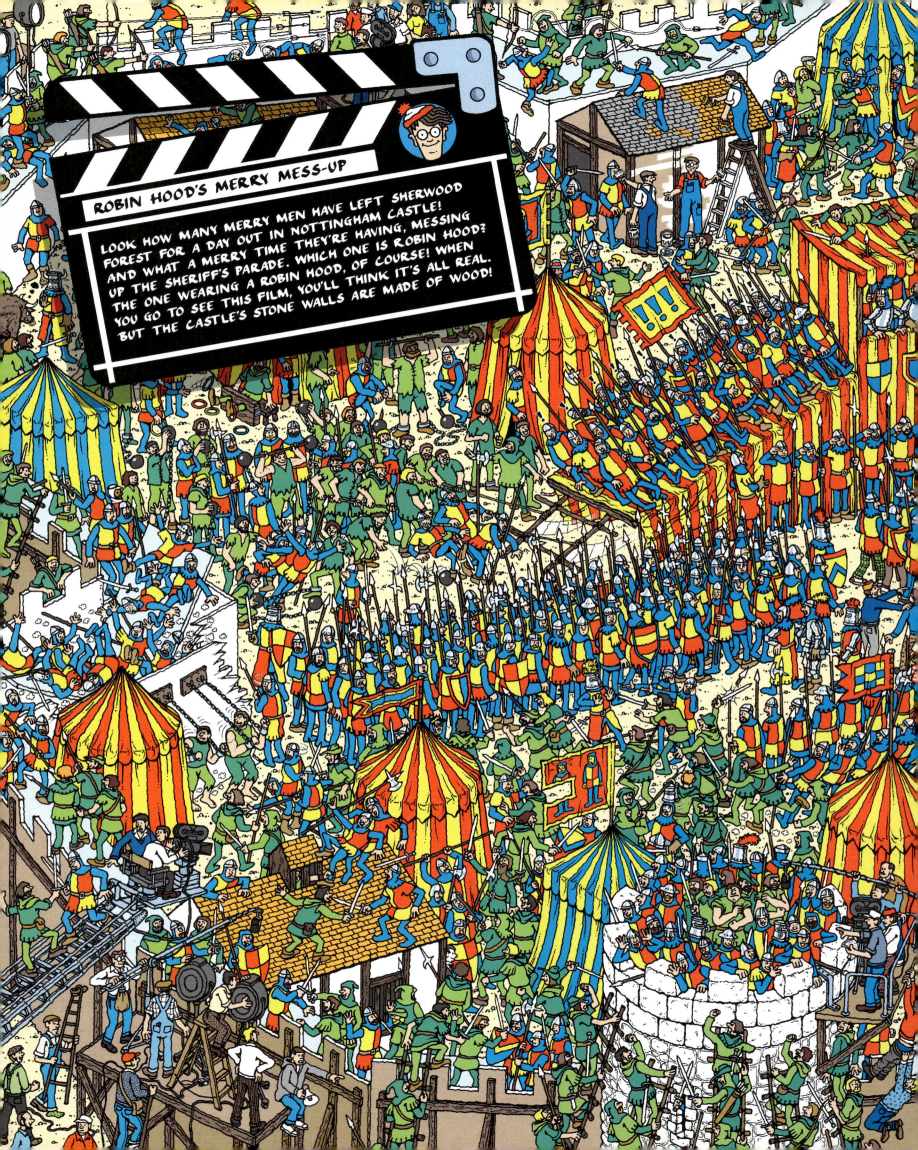

ROBIN HOOD'S MERRY MESS-UP

LOOK HOW MANY MERRY MEN HAVE LEFT SHERWOOD
FOREST FOR A DAY OUT IN NOTTINGHAM CASTLE!
AND WHAT A MERRY TIME THEY'RE HAVING, MESSING
UP THE SHERIFF'S PARADE. WHICH ONE IS ROBIN HOOD?
THE ONE WEARING A ROBIN HOOD, OF COURSE! WHEN
YOU GO TO SEE THIS FILM, YOU'LL THINK IT'S ALL REAL,
BUT THE CASTLE'S STONE WALLS ARE MADE OF WOOD!

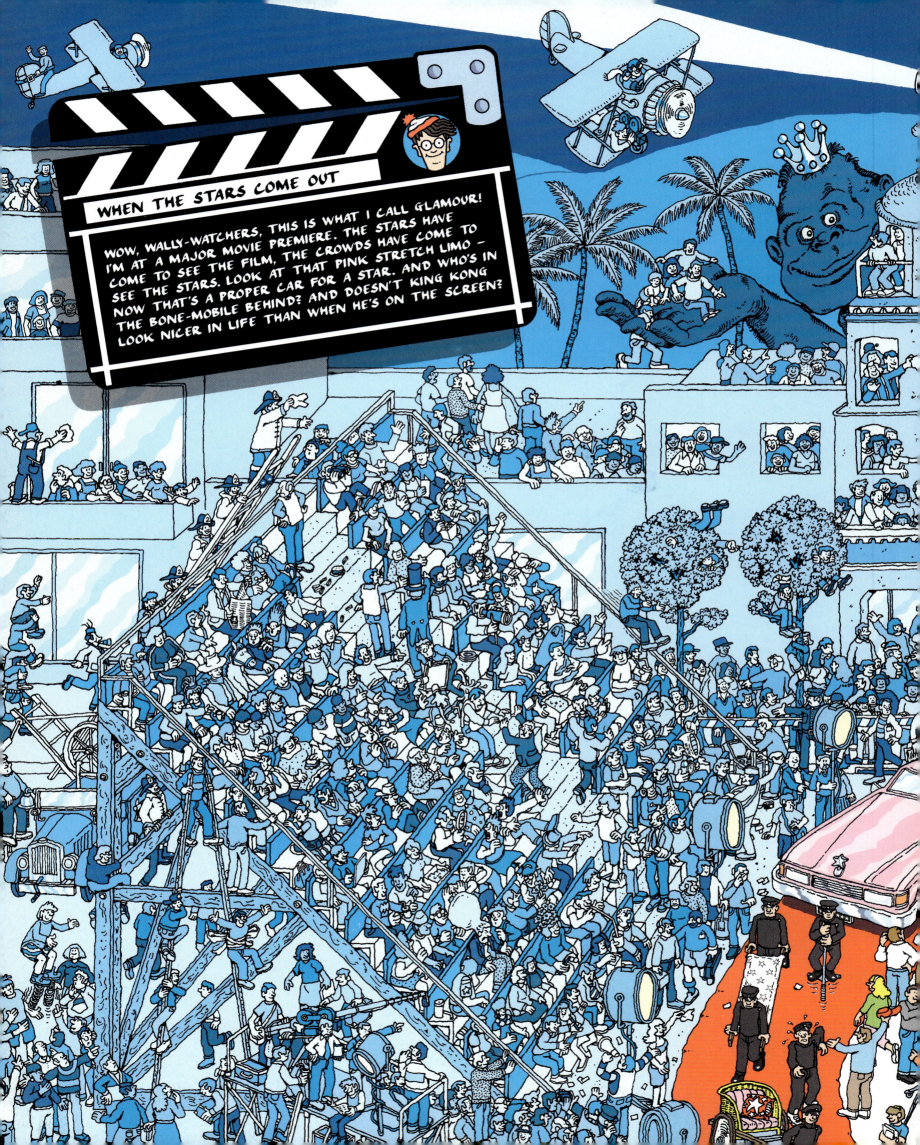

WHEN THE STARS COME OUT

WOW, WALLY-WATCHERS, THIS IS WHAT I CALL GLAMOUR!
I'M AT A MAJOR MOVIE PREMIERE. THE STARS HAVE
COME TO SEE THE FILM, THE CROWDS HAVE COME TO
SEE THE STARS. LOOK AT THAT PINK STRETCH LIMO –
NOW THAT'S A PROPER CAR FOR A STAR. AND WHO'S IN
THE BONE-MOBILE BEHIND? AND DOESN'T KING KONG
LOOK NICER IN LIFE THAN WHEN HE'S ON THE SCREEN?

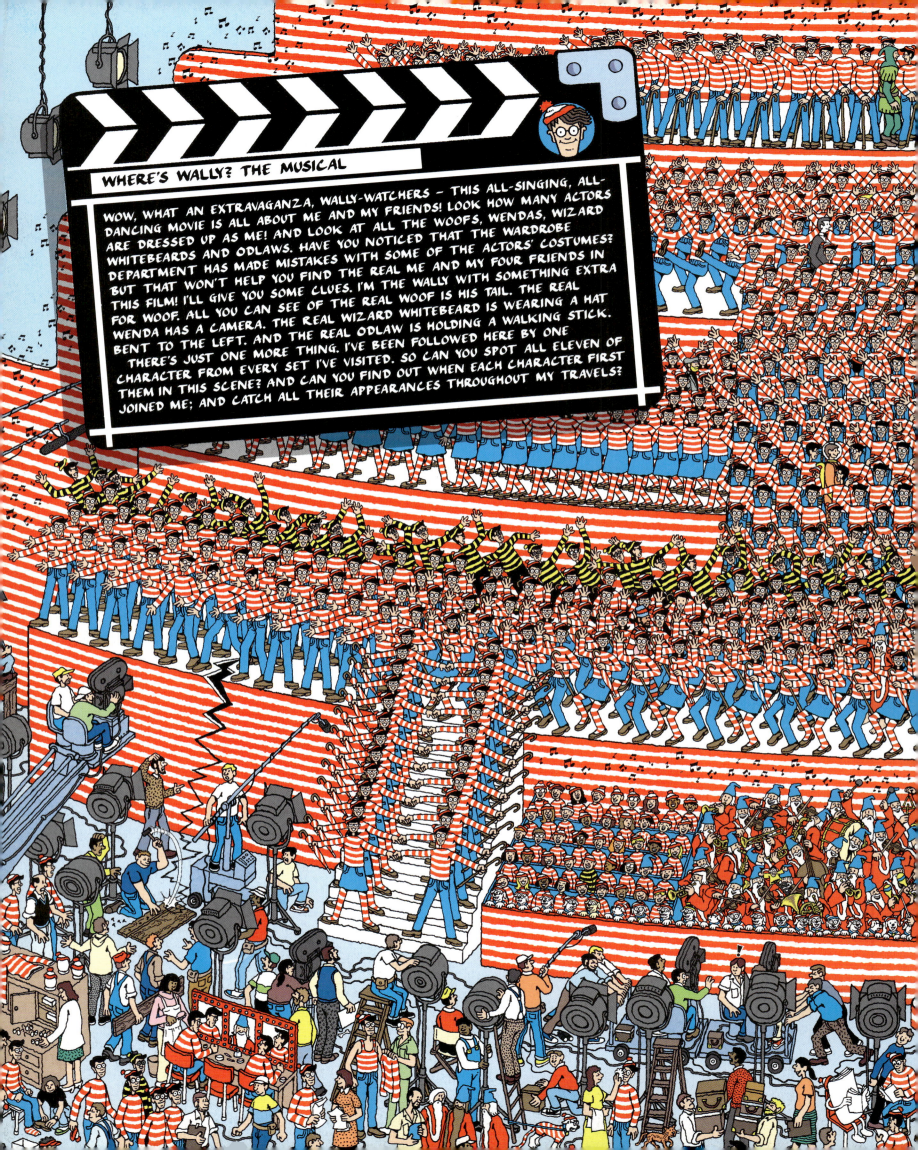

WHERE'S WALLY? THE MUSICAL

WOW, WHAT AN EXTRAVAGANZA, WALLY-WATCHERS – THIS ALL-SINGING, ALL-DANCING MOVIE IS ALL ABOUT ME AND MY FRIENDS! LOOK HOW MANY ACTORS ARE DRESSED UP AS ME! AND LOOK AT ALL THE WOOFS, WENDAS, WIZARD WHITEBEARDS AND ODLAWS. HAVE YOU NOTICED THAT THE WARDROBE DEPARTMENT HAS MADE MISTAKES WITH SOME OF THE ACTORS' COSTUMES? BUT THAT WON'T HELP YOU FIND THE REAL ME AND MY FOUR FRIENDS IN THIS FILM! I'LL GIVE YOU SOME CLUES. I'M THE WALLY WITH SOMETHING EXTRA FOR WOOF. ALL YOU CAN SEE OF THE REAL WOOF IS HIS TAIL. THE REAL WENDA HAS A CAMERA. THE REAL WIZARD WHITEBEARD IS WEARING A HAT BENT TO THE LEFT. AND THE REAL ODLAW IS HOLDING A WALKING STICK.

THERE'S JUST ONE MORE THING. I'VE BEEN FOLLOWED HERE BY ONE CHARACTER FROM EVERY SET I'VE VISITED. SO CAN YOU SPOT ALL ELEVEN OF THEM IN THIS SCENE? AND CAN YOU FIND OUT WHEN EACH CHARACTER FIRST JOINED ME; AND CATCH ALL THEIR APPEARANCES THROUGHOUT MY TRAVELS?

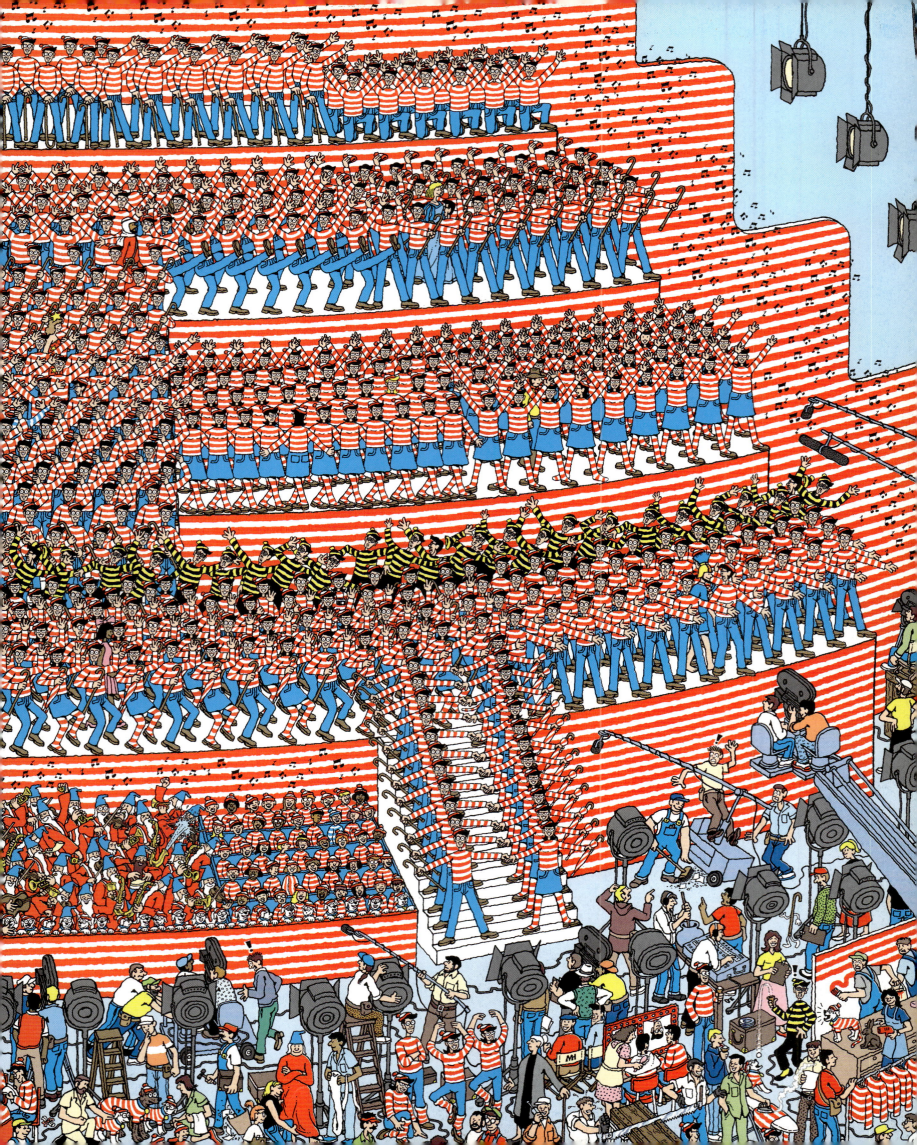

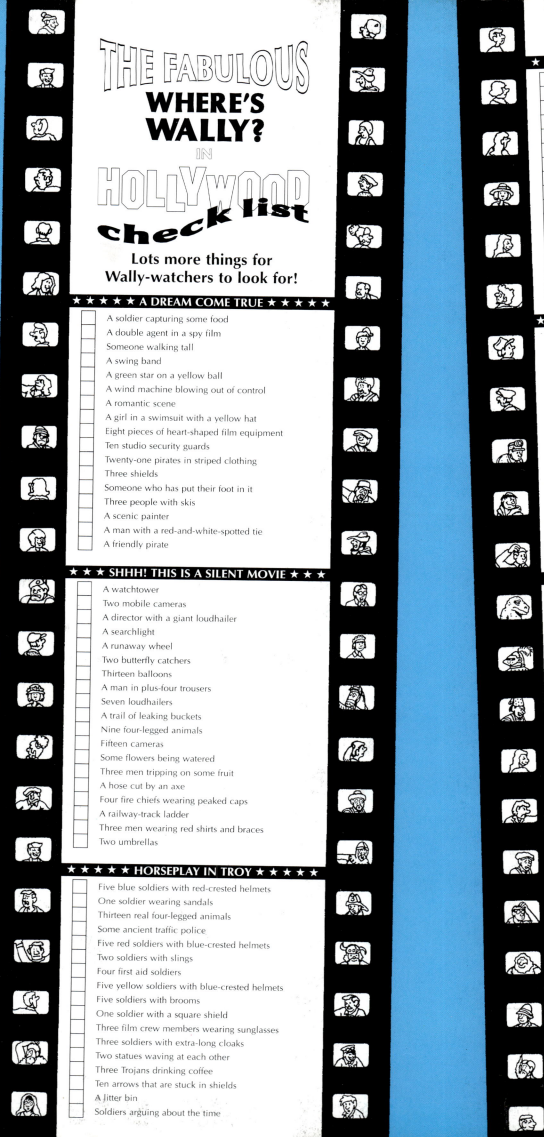

THE FABULOUS WHERE'S WALLY? IN HOLLYWOOD

check list

Lots more things for Wally-watchers to look for!

★ ★ ★ ★ A DREAM COME TRUE ★ ★ ★ ★

- A soldier capturing some food
- A double agent in a spy film
- Someone walking tall
- A swing band
- A green star on a yellow ball
- A wind machine blowing out of control
- A romantic scene
- A girl in a swimsuit with a yellow hat
- Eight pieces of heart-shaped film equipment
- Ten studio security guards
- Twenty-one pirates in striped clothing
- Three shields
- Someone who has put their foot in it
- Three people with skis
- A scenic painter
- A man with a red-and-white-spotted tie
- A friendly pirate

★ ★ ★ SHHH! THIS IS A SILENT MOVIE ★ ★ ★

- A watchtower
- Two mobile cameras
- A director with a giant loudhailer
- A searchlight
- A runaway wheel
- Two butterfly catchers
- Thirteen balloons
- A man in plus-four trousers
- Seven loudhailers
- A trail of leaking buckets
- Nine four-legged animals
- Fifteen cameras
- Some flowers being watered
- Three men tripping on some fruit
- A hose cut by an axe
- Four fire chiefs wearing peaked caps
- A railway-track ladder
- Three men wearing red shirts and braces
- Two umbrellas

★ ★ ★ ★ HORSEPLAY IN TROY ★ ★ ★ ★

- Five blue soldiers with red-crested helmets
- One soldier wearing sandals
- Thirteen real four-legged animals
- Some ancient traffic police
- Five red soldiers with blue-crested helmets
- Two soldiers with slings
- Four first aid soldiers
- Five yellow soldiers with blue-crested helmets
- Five soldiers with brooms
- One soldier with a square shield
- Three film crew members wearing sunglasses
- Three soldiers with extra-long cloaks
- Two statues waving at each other
- Three Trojans drinking coffee
- Ten arrows that are stuck in shields
- A litter bin
- Soldiers arguing about the time

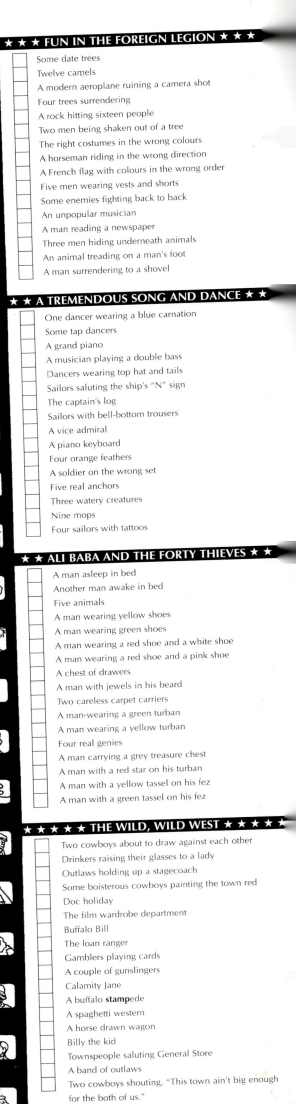

★ ★ ★ FUN IN THE FOREIGN LEGION ★ ★ ★

- Some date trees
- Twelve camels
- A modern aeroplane ruining a camera shot
- Four trees surrendering
- A rock hitting sixteen people
- Two men being shaken out of a tree
- The right costumes in the wrong colours
- A horseman riding in the wrong direction
- A French flag with colours in the wrong order
- Five men wearing vests and shorts
- Some enemies fighting back to back
- An unpopular musician
- A man reading a newspaper
- Three men hiding underneath animals
- An animal treading on a man's foot
- A man surrendering to a shovel

★ ★ A TREMENDOUS SONG AND DANCE ★ ★

- One dancer wearing a blue carnation
- Some tap dancers
- A grand piano
- A musician playing a double bass
- Dancers wearing top hat and tails
- Sailors saluting the ship's "N" sign
- The captain's log
- Sailors with bell-bottom trousers
- A vice admiral
- A piano keyboard
- Four orange feathers
- A soldier on the wrong set
- Five real anchors
- Three watery creatures
- Nine mops
- Four sailors with tattoos

★ ★ ALI BABA AND THE FORTY THIEVES ★ ★

- A man asleep in bed
- Another man awake in bed
- Five animals
- A man wearing yellow shoes
- A man wearing green shoes
- A man wearing a red shoe and a white shoe
- A man wearing a red shoe and a pink shoe
- A chest of drawers
- A man with jewels in his beard
- Two careless carpet carriers
- A man-wearing a green turban
- A man wearing a yellow turban
- Four real genies
- A man carrying a grey treasure chest
- A man with a red star on his turban
- A man with a yellow tassel on his fez
- A man with a green tassel on his fez

★ ★ ★ ★ THE WILD, WILD WEST ★ ★ ★ ★

- Two cowboys about to draw against each other
- Drinkers raising their glasses to a lady
- Outlaws holding up a stagecoach
- Some boisterous cowboys painting the town red
- Doc holiday
- The film wardrobe department
- Buffalo Bill
- The loan ranger
- Gamblers playing cards
- A couple of gunslingers
- Calamity Jane
- A buffalo **stamp**ede
- A spaghetti western
- A horse drawn wagon
- Billy the kid
- Townspeople saluting General Store
- A band of outlaws
- Two cowboys shouting, "This town ain't big enough for the both of us."